GW00702238

THE SILENCE OF
SOUND MIRRORS

Charlotte

Best whishes, from Pauline

THE
SILENCE
OF
SOUND
MIRRORS

Poems by
PAULINE STAINER

Illustrations by
ROSAMOND ULPH

ORPHEAN PRESS

2021

First published in 2021 by Orphean Press
10 Heath Close, Polstead Heath, Colchester CO6 5BE

ORPHEAN

PRESS

Typeset in 16- on 21-point ITC Golden Cockerel
and printed in Great Britain by Peter Newble:
10 Heath Close, Polstead Heath, Colchester CO6 5BE
peter @ newble . com ∻ www . newble . com

2021

Bound by Flyleaf Ltd, Kirby Cross, Frinton-on-Sea CO 13 0PG
www . flyleaf . co . uk

ISBN *978-1-908198-22-8*
Text © Pauline Stainer
Illustrations © Rosamond Ulph
All rights reserved

No part of this publication may be produced, stored in a private re-
trieval system, or transmitted, in any form or by any means without the
prior permission in writing of the author, nor otherwise be circulated in
any form or binding or cover than that in which it is published and
without a similar condition, including this condition, being imposed on
the subsequent purchaser.

British Library Cataloguing in Publication Data
A catalogue record for this book is available from the British Library.

CONTENTS

The silence of sound mirrors   *page* 1

The tremor   3

Thresholds   5

Marsh orchids   7

Sea-glass   9

Saltmarsh   11

The etching   13

Flux   15

Watertower   17

The rustle of time   19

Passing through   21

Pilgrimage   23

The word and the moment   25

Biographies   26

THE SILENCE OF
SOUND MIRRORS

They never worked
leant into the wind
or sleepwalked
like standing stones

but their curving abstracts
still linger along the coast
throwing the shadow
of unauthorised gods

even now, hoar frost
on their spherical mirrors
dumbfounds us,
like snow

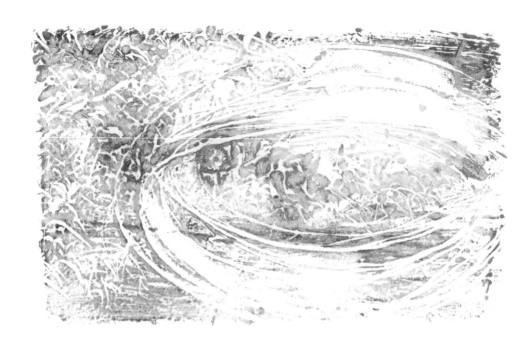

THE TREMOR

I glimpsed them backlit
in winter sun,
white fallow deer
resting

and in that moment
of perfect hesitation
a wind shivered
the blackthorn blossom

THRESHOLDS

Dewfall on deep furrow
flaxen owl above
a flowing field

blue intake of breath
at the silken hem
of the tide

MARSH ORCHIDS

Rust on corrugated iron
in the iron-red gulley

rocks brilliant green
with oxidised copper ore

pollen residues
in abandoned places

marsh orchids beside
rainwater hollows

mantle of moss
thickening, thickening

SEA-GLASS

Bloom of sea-glass
on shingle

celadon green
subtler than willow

blue of reindeer eyes
in winter

sanguine glass
salt-glazed

weight of memory
water-worn

the strange beauty
of attrition

SALTMARSH

The plane sank slowly

no wreckage visible
until things worked
to the surface

pollens settling
on interplay
of water and light

sudden birds
singing through rain,
silence from the cockpit

slippage,
the dark underside
of the heart

THE ETCHING

Utter renewal,
to etch sunlight
on driftwood

the dunes humming between tides
visitation of salt
along the shingle spit

inspiration
the flicker of a bird
into the heart

FLUX

I stood beyond quicksands
on the slatted bridge,
the river flowing out
as the sea crept in

strange, that sense of the eternal
when even the heart lies down,
the estuary still wearing
the moon at its throat

WATERTOWER

Ruinous,
only swallows in the rafters
above the watertank,
the late summer
hectic with their heartbeats,
throats escutcheoned
against the deepening dusk

THE RUSTLE OF TIME

It caught our breath

not the sudden bank
of bluebells
but a torched car
in the holloway

burnt roof fallen in,
rusted springs
scrambled like tree roots
between blackthorn, elm sapling

the skeletal steering wheel
still under wildcrab blossom

PASSING THROUGH

We crossed the dry river
under a blood-wolf moon
stepping-stones still
flashing their flint

bare earth,
burnt red,
the alchemy
of drought

and the otherness
of a dawn chorus
from ancient tamarisk trees

PILGRIMAGE

Long after the war
we went back
to the sea cemetery

the dead laid
under great spearheads
of cumulus

shingle waves, wild goats,
the blue murmur
of islands between tides

THE WORD AND
THE MOMENT

I had scrambled up
the high ridge
to explore the great cavern
with its overhang
of softening purples

no ancient pollen
or subsong of birds,
simply something withheld,
the listening silence
of rain shadow

BIOGRAPHIES

Pauline Stainer has published nine collections of poetry with Bloodaxe. She was awarded a Hawthornden Fellowship, and has worked with artists before, notably the Brotherhood of Ruralists.

Rosamond Ulph works as an artist within a wide range of media including calligraphic maps, botanical art and book illustrations. This is the second publication on which she and Pauline Stainer have worked together.